DECISIONS
that
DEFINE US

a journey of transformation

DAVID CRONE
FOREWORD BY BILL JOHNSON

All Scripture references are from the following sources:

The New International Version of the Bible (NIV) © 1984 by the International Bible Society.

The New King James Version (NKJV) © 1979, 1980, 1982, 1992, Thomas Nelson, Inc., Publisher.

I wish to acknowledge the community of friends at The Mission that have given us room to adventure in the Spirit. They have demonstrated great patience and a willingness to trust when they didn't understand. May they inherit all the promises that come with faith and patience (Heb. 6:12).

I want to thank Joyce Milton, Katherine Martin, and Dan McCollam for freely volunteering their time and incredible gifts in editing this book into a readable story and bringing it to print.

Contents

Foreword

Introduction

1. Decisions that Define Us   15

2. The Shift is On   23

3. The House that God Built.   29

4. Points of No Return   37

5. Dreams and Visions   49

6. "You Need Her"   55

7. Contending for the Call   65

8. Authentic Christianity   71

9. A New Team Paradigm   81

10. The Sign Out by the Street   93

11. Friends   103

12. Dreaming with God   111

13. The Decisions and You   119

14. Therefore...   125

Foreword

The Church is in a season of major transition. Everywhere you turn there are individuals and groups making changes thought to be nearly impossible. Believers are crying out for more of God in ways they once renounced. And it's not always because they received more correct teaching, although that sometimes plays a role. It's usually because deep within their hearts, there is an uncontrollable cry that is born of the Spirit of God. It is the Holy Spirit who has ignited these birth pangs. This movement of the Holy Spirit is the deep of God calling to the deep of man.

Desperation does strange things to people. Imagine a timid young mother in a mall catching a man who is trying to take her newborn child. She is timid no longer. Instead she takes on the characteristics of a mother bear defending her cubs. And woe to the man who falls prey to her anger. In like manner people are stepping outside of their comfort zones and pursuing God with reckless abandon. Such actions get Heaven's attention.

The pursuit of Kingdom experiences is legitimate and justified. The philosophy of Christianity will no longer satisfy. We must encounter Him. But to do so without gaining a transformed mind in the process is really to miss the point. Kingdom perspective is one of the rarest and most valuable commodities in all the world. It alone can accomplish what our hearts cry out for, and it positions us to change the course of world history.

David Crone's book, Decisions that Define Us, is a book written with this in mind. He brilliantly targets the heart to transform the mind. Anyone who ponders over the revelations on these pages and boldly says "yes" to God will be launched on an irreversible journey of personal transformation. And only transformed people can become transformers.

I highly recommend this book in the same way that I highly recommend the messenger. The Crones are some of our dearest friends and partners in life and ministry. I celebrate the fact that this book was first lived, and then put in print.

Bill Johnson, Senior Leader
Bethel Church, Redding, California

Introduction

In 1996, I didn't even know I was in a rut. I'd learned about the gifts of the Spirit and how to pastor them wisely in Bible School, where we were taught an unspoken code that would help us protect people from weird teaching and behavior. Our denomination was a great movement born at the turn of the last century out of the Azusa Street Revival. We studied Pentecostal history from a "we've come a long way, baby" perspective, and graduated skilled at preparing three-point sermons with good illustrations. We believed that the gifts of the Spirit, including speaking in tongues, were still important for Christians today, but many of our churches had a layer of "sophistication" covering our radical roots.

Twenty-four years after I entered full-time ministry, I still enjoyed being a normal pastor and loved the people; it was a good fit. If I lived in a box, it was a comfortable, moral box.

Then we began to hear stories about a broad sweep of refreshing that stirred in many an increased spiritual passion—and a whole bunch of weird behavior. We heard about churches where people shook violently and were frequently "slain in the Spirit". Many were finding new joy that was demonstrated by long periods of laughter. Honestly, to someone walking in from the street, it probably looked like some people had developed serious "tics" as they jerked their heads and uttered strange-sounding grunts and groans.

Many pastors were being hit with fresh fire and behaved just as unpredictably as their congregations. I couldn't figure out why this was necessary. After all, we already believed in and practiced the gifts of the Spirit. When my wife Deborah and I discussed the unsettling reports we heard during those early days, I repeatedly said, "If this is a move of God…" I honestly wasn't sure.

If I was leery, Deborah processed these first stories like a lawyer listening to an opposing attorney in an important court case. Inside, she was waving wildly, shouting, "I object!" Deb had recently experienced the unexpected loss of her father and was going through a season when her heavenly Father was challenging the way she thought about Him. This was a spiritually and emotionally draining time for her; the last thing she needed was a bunch of emotional people looking for an experience. At least she felt that way until she began to encounter the Holy Spirit in a new way herself.

It Only Felt Like Death

Today we can see that what looked like a massive change in our attitudes and behavior was actually a process of being restored to the way we were created. Even when we still viewed the increased move of the Holy Spirit with great caution, our hearts were hungry for a more challenging walk with God. If it was real and of God, we wanted it—without limits.

Ultimately, we chose to go after God with all our hearts, in whatever way He made Himself known, come heaven or high water. In the face of a growing body of evidence that we could no longer ignore, we set out on a journey of exploration, feeling like Edmund and Lucy when they stepped through the wardrobe into the land of Narnia. A dear pastor friend of ours described our exploration this way: "David and Deborah walked to the edge of the cliff and looked down at the river below. They joined hands, looked at each other and without hesitation, jumped."

We paid a high and painful price for this commitment in the months and years to come. When I use the word we, I am referring not only to the leadership, but to the entire congregation, those that stayed and those that felt they needed to leave. The gradual reclamation of our church by the Spirit of God has been like an ebbing, flowing ocean. As each wave hit, folks would leave the church, in part because things at every level of church life were changing and becoming unfamiliar. The very structure and values of the church were in transition, which left people with little safe ground to stand on. The Holy Spirit was not letting us get comfortable.

Reconstruction is Messy

Several years ago Deborah and I took on the challenge of building our own home. For many months I would head to the office in my suit and Deb would head to the work site in overalls. After my time at the office, I would join her and we would work until late in the night. One of the difficulties during that time was that we had to live with the chaos created by the building process. Our schedules, our living conditions, even the way we related to each other had to be adjusted on the run, putting pressure on every part of our lives.

This is a good picture of what was happening in the church. God was disorienting our lives in order to reorient them. This was an exciting time for many of us, but we found that not everyone could—or wanted to—live in the atmosphere of transition. They needed something more secure and safe, and we were anything but that.

Since my heart remains, first and foremost, the heart of a local pastor, watching people leave the church was excruciating. I soon discovered that my pastoral experience did not serve me well in this season, which made this time even more bewildering. Through the fire of these trying times, however, the values that have defined the church began to take shape. They ultimately became declarations that I read aloud for the first time at the graduation of our Potter's House School of the Supernatural in May 2004.

Since then, they have circulated globally via the Internet, resonating within the hearts of leaders around the world. Many have called or written to ask permission to use these decisions in their local churches.

Stories, not Slogans

This book is a result of our desire to help leaders contextualize these decisions so that they don't simply attempt to adopt them as slogans. To help you internalize these powerful concepts—to make them more real and help you understand their cost—I'll tell you some of the stories we lived through in order to reach them.

One last bit of fine print: The stories about the journey of The Mission are told from Deborah's and my perspective. Like all perspectives, ours is determined in large part by the color of the lens we see through and the influence of the people around us. It is at best imperfect. I am confident that there are others whose point of view is quite different, and just as valid. However, I present these stories without apology, and hope that our perspective will be helpful in your journey.

As you read these stories, I'd like to ask you to do me a favor. Would you take a little time to make this book your journey, not just mine? At the end of each chapter, you'll find a question or two, with space for you to journal your thoughts, if you like.

chapter
1

DECISIONS THAT DEFINE US

B efore you read these decisions it is important for you to understand the context. These are not and never were a reaction to anything but the state of our own hearts and the reality in our church. They are absolutely in no way a criticism of any church or denominational movement. We are in this battle for high ground together: one Church, one Bride, one Body.

We would probably have said these decisions were true from the beginning of our ministry. Now, however, they are points of contention, foundational values without which we are not willing to live.

In II Samuel 6, as David leads the return of the Ark of the Covenant, there is both celebration and sacrifice; and so it is with these commitments. As we are heeding the ever-increasing call to clear a path for the manifest presence and glory of God, these decisions have each taken a piece out of our hearts and lives, and given us something priceless in return.

Mile Markers

These are not arrogant proclamations of our accomplishments;

they are fresh commitments to Jesus' teachings and actions. There is still so much more ground to contend for. We continue to comprehend the high cost and great value of each declaration of purpose, while remaining humbly aware that Jesus paid the price that made possible the events of the Book of Acts—then and now

So, then, here are the Decisions that Define Us:

- We have decided that teaching the gospel without demonstrating the gospel is not enough. Good preaching, good doctrine, and being good people are not enough.

- We have decided that having a good church club is not enough, good fellowship is not enough, and just being a member of that club is not enough.

- We have decided that having good Bible studies is good, but not good enough, that just making it to heaven is not our goal, and that knowing about God without truly knowing and experiencing God is meaningless.

- We have decided that having good programs is not enough, that change without transformation is intolerable, and that staying where we are is not an option.

- We have decided that gifting without character is futile.

- We have decided that singing songs without worshiping is empty, and having meetings without God showing up is pointless.

- We have decided that having faith without works

is not enough and having works without love is not acceptable—that our function comes out of our relationship first with the Father and second with each other.

- We have decided that reading about the book of Acts without living the book of Acts is unthinkable.

- We have decided that confident faith is good and bold faith is better.

- We have decided that hearing about the Holy Spirit without experiencing Him is silly, that believing in His presence without seeing it manifested in signs and wonders is hypocrisy, that believing in healing without seeing people healed is absurd, and that believing in deliverance without people being delivered is absolutely ridiculous.

- We have decided to be Holy Spirit filled, Holy Spirit led, and Holy Spirit empowered—anything less doesn't work for us.

- We have decided to be the ones telling the stories of God's power—not the ones hearing about them.

- We have decided that living saved but not supernatural is living below our privilege and short of what Christ died for.

- We have decided that we are a battle ship not a cruise ship, an army not an audience, Special Forces not spectators, missionaries not club members.

- We have decided to value both pioneers and settlers: pioneers to expand our territory and settlers to build on those territories. But we are not squatters, people who take up space others have fought for without improving it.

- We have decided to be infectious instead of innocuous, contagious instead of quarantine, deadly instead of benign.

- We have decided to be radical lovers and outrageous givers.

- We have decided that we are a mission station and not a museum.

- We have decided that it is better to fail while reaching for the impossible that God has planned for us than to succeed settling for less.

- We have decided that nothing short of His Kingdom coming and His will being done in our world as it is in heaven will satisfy.

- We have decided that we will not be satisfied until our world cries out, "Those who have turned the world upside down have come here too" (Acts 17:6, NKJV).

These are some of the decisions that define who we are as a community and how we choose to live our lives.

These decisions are not destinations, but rather journeys—journeys along an ancient path. We have not found some new way. We discovered an avenue as old as Abraham, Isaac and Jacob, traveled by Moses, Joshua and Caleb. On this same risky road, Paul, John, and Peter paved the way for the first century church, a church that revolutionized the culture of the first century and beyond.

It is an adventure that will impact our world today. It is a path of *Bold Faith*—believing that what God says is really true and acting on it; *Outrageous Generosity*—giving our life away in order to demonstrate His Kingdom; *Radical Love*—loving God with everything in us and our neighbor as ourselves.

It is a life of liberty, freedom, and healing, where you will find significance, purpose, and destiny. This is a path less traveled. However, it is not a journey available only to a select few; anyone may come on this highway cut by the hand of God for people of every nation, tribe and tongue, for those in any occupation or vocation.

No matter where you are in your life journey, there is room on this path for you.

Reflection Questions:

If these decisions resonate with you, you're a leader. Whether God has called you to influence your co-workers, your family, your friends, or a church community, this book was written for you.

Which decisions were the most meaningful to you? Did you make any notes in the margin as you read though them? If not, you might want to take time to do that before you go any further.

chapter
2

THE SHIFT IS ON

"We have decided that it is better to fail while reaching for the impossible that God has planned for us than to succeed settling for less."

Deb and I were watching a baseball game one day when Barry Bonds came up to bat. The announcer said, "Well, the shift is on." Sure enough, everyone in the infield had moved away from their usual positions, hoping to stop the power hitter from getting on base.

Times of shifting are described throughout the Bible. Isaiah 54:2 puts it this way: "Enlarge the place of your tent, stretch your tent curtains wide, do not hold back; lengthen your cords, strengthen your stakes" (NIV). Jesus spoke of a shift when he said to the woman at the well, "The hour is coming, and now is, when the true worshipers will worship the Father in spirit and truth" (John 4:23, NKJV). You'll notice significant times of shifting right from the beginning of the stories that led us to The Decisions.

Facing My Fears

One of my personal struggles as a young man was living with a fear of failure. For most of my life I made decisions based on my ability to perform. If failure was a possibility I would find a reason not to try. This way of dealing with the possibility of failure continued as I grew older, and it affected my total approach to life—including ministry. I got rather good at masking the true excuse for my decisions by using logic that sounded spiritually reasonable. In fact, I was so good at it that I usually failed to recognize it and often called the decisions I made wisdom and an act of faith. The truth is that it was the wisdom of man and that my faith was captive to a huge calculator—one that wouldn't let me step into the realm of risk.

My World is Shaken

Often, times of major shifting can be traced to a single event. This was true for me as my personal paradigm really started to shift when the Holy Spirit chose to surprise me in a store, of all places.

While in a Celtic shop browsing through notebooks full of historic crests, I came upon a family motto that stirred me deeply. When I called Deborah over and began to read the commitment to her, my knees buckled. I had to hold onto the counter to remain standing as I finished reading aloud the mission statement behind the Buchan family crest. These were the words that impacted me:

Non Inferiora Secutus

"Not having followed inferior things"

The whole picture unfolded in an instant. I saw the fact that this wasn't just a nice slogan: the Buchan family had chosen a radical foundation from which to make their decisions.

We went outside and I tried to catch my breath. Leaning against a lamppost, hardly able to stand, I exclaimed to

Deborah, "Can you believe that? This family chose to make the pursuit of excellence their life message. They were determined to make it their legacy, regardless of the cost." Deborah realized I was being emotionally wrecked by this revelation and she enjoyed watching the download.

Believe me, the effect of that encounter went far beyond my emotions; I had found the words that verbalized the cry of my heart. I became painfully aware that the basis for my decisions had to change; there was no other option. For the sake of my own spiritual life, the destiny of my family, and the health of the church, this motto had to become my reality.

Well, the shift was on.

New Rings for a New Covenant

Over the next few months, I presented our sons and my son-in-law with signet rings engraved with the acronym NIS (for Non Inferiora Secutus), along with a family pledge that Deb and I had crafted: "The wearers of these rings covenant together to never walk in inferior paths, choose inferior goals, or settle for inferior character. Each will aspire, with the help of God and each other, to reach for the greatest good in all things pertaining to faith and life."

When Deb had my ring engraved, she picked it up from the engraver and was startled when our son-in-law asked, "Mom, why did they engrave Dad's ring with 'SIN'?" The engravers had not reversed the letters; Bryant was simply reading the ring backwards. "NIS" turned upside down reads "SIN". When Deb related the story to me I was immediately reminded of the passage that states: "To him who knows to do good and does not do it, to him it is sin" (James 4:17, NKJV). This revelation strengthened our commitment to live with a new set of decisions.

This personal shift set us on a journey that began to impact everything around us, including the church. Throughout this journey we have been marked painfully many times by the actions of people who didn't understand our decisions and judged only our mistakes. God required us to remain very vulnerable and open as we explored new paths in unexplored territory. Along the way He has also marked us with His incredible grace, a gift that has given us courage to continue to believe that destiny is more important than that which looks like success.

Reflection Questions:

Does your family have a crest or motto, promise or significant scripture passage to live by? What does the Buchan family crest, NIS, speak to you?

chapter
3

THE HOUSE
THAT GOD BUILT

"We have decided that confident faith is good and bold faith is better."

"We have decided to be radical lovers and outrageous givers."

"Building Program"—those might be two of the most dreaded words in a pastor's vocabulary. We needed to build a new sanctuary, and I'd never led a church through that process, but I had witnessed enough others going through it to discourage me. Many of my ministry colleagues had taken on the task, only to resign in complete exhaustion when the building was complete. The fundraising technique I had observed seemed more like a cheesy marketing scheme than the strategy of the Kingdom of God. I expected to hear an announcer say, "And for just $19.99 you also get…"

My lack of enthusiasm to build was encouraged by our church's history. The building of the original structures on our present site had left the church in such heavy debt that ministries were restricted and staff underpaid. The weight of the financial bondage affected everything in the church. Along with this difficulty, on three occasions in the past, architectural drawings had been drawn up and paid for. Each time, attempts were made to raise the funds to build a large sanctuary in order to complete the original plan for our campus. Each effort ended in frustration and discouragement.

Searching for a New Model

Despite this history, the Lord was beginning to make it clear that He wanted the sanctuary built. Realizing this, Deborah and I—along with the church board—committed ourselves to see it happen God's way, completely free from the manipulation of human hands. Deb and I often wistfully wondered, "Is it possible that there is a place where a church building could be erected that is not marred by the fingerprints of man, leaving the church in a place of freedom rather than financial bondage? And is it possible that Vacaville could be that place?" We moved forward with the hope in our heart that the answer was a divine "Yes". The journey became quite interesting.

In 1997, a couple of our staff pastors and I attended Tommy Barnett's annual Pastors' Conference in Phoenix, anxious to be exposed once again to Tommy's gigantic heart and infectious faith.

We listened intently as he presented a new ministry—the Dream Center—his church was sponsoring in Los Angeles. The center would be led by Tommy's son Matthew, and promised to have a great impact on many people who were bound by various addictions. I knew the Holy Spirit was prompting me to give something to the Dream Center.

Deborah and I have always loved joyous, obedient giving, so hearing from God about an offering was nothing new. I went to pray up on their Prayer Hill after one of the sessions.

An Amazing Answer

I heard these words: "All of it." I immediately realized that God was talking about the money the church had put aside for the new sanctuary, a sum of $120,000. That was a lot of money to us, and it had taken several months to accumulate. I knew I was hearing from God, and I knew He was serious. This divine appointment at Prayer Hill marked the beginning of a different era for me. I was called to function in the word of knowledge as God gave me instructions and tested my faith to a totally new level. I wasn't getting any direction that was even vaguely safe: either I was hearing the Holy Spirit or I wasn't. But He soon assured me that I wasn't walking alone, by using something personal to me to confirm this new path.

There on Prayer Hill and throughout the rest of the afternoon, one of my favorite hymns, Great is Thy Faithfulness, echoed in my mind and heart. That night, as Tommy prepared to receive the offering and faith promises for the Dream Center, I gathered my courage and wrote a brief message on a pledge card. "$120,000.00—Tommy, please call me." I have never been more fearful in the midst of an act of faith as I was in that moment. Then just as I dropped the pledge card in the offering basket, the choir and orchestra broke into a chorus of Great is Thy Faithfulness. The memory of that moment would hold me in the place of faith during the testing months ahead.

There are so many more chapters in the sanctuary story; in fact, it's another book in itself. But I can't go on without telling you one more faith-stretching experience.

God's Time Frame

When we presented that check to Tommy Barnett, God said to me, "Within a year, you'll be ready to begin building." I knew what that meant. As part of keeping the building project free from human manipulation, we felt strongly that we were to pay cash as we built. To do that, we needed to have $1,000,000 in the bank to start the project.

God definitely upped the ante when He asked me to believe that we would have that much in the bank within a year. Well, to make a long story very short, we verified a $1,000,000 bank account balance on the one-year anniversary—to the day—of God's million-dollar promise. As you can imagine, when we stand and worship in a 37,000 square foot sanctuary that was completed on time and in cash, it's a sign and a wonder. There were so many forks in the road where it would have been much easier to put our human hands on the process, but the Holy Spirit was faithful to consistently call us to do things His way.

Wise Words

Even as I am writing this chapter I am reflecting on a significant moment in time before the building project began. Deborah and I had just become the senior pastor of what is now The Mission. It was Christmas Eve and we were sitting around the table in our home eating clam chowder and crab cioppino. With us were our dear friends and mentors, Paul and Margaret Schoch, along with an 85-year-old pastor from England. We had the sense that we were sitting with the Apostles. At an unexpected moment, Paul turned to me and said, "David, your job is not to pastor this church, but to hear from the Holy Spirit and do what He tells you." The conversation continued on, but those words were all I could think about for the rest of the evening—really for the rest of my life.

I believe it was in that moment a new journey began, an adventure based on the mindset that I would settle for nothing less than walking in daily fellowship with the Holy Spirit.

Reflection Questions:

Are you remembering a faith-stretching time in your own life? Perhaps you've heard from God but you haven't responded with obedience yet. Whatever the case, here's a place to write your thoughts before you go on to the next chapter.

chapter
4

POINTS OF NO RETURN

"We have decided that having a good church club is not enough, good fellowship is not enough, and just being a member of that club is not enough."

"We have decided that just making it to heaven is not our goal, and that knowing about God without truly knowing and experiencing God is meaningless."

Telling the story of "the house that God built" never gets old. But there's another path that runs parallel to the physical building process: the road of rebuilding the internal structure of the church.

God didn't give us a blueprint or an outline to follow for this upgrade. All we knew was that we were committed to doing church God's way. Mistakes? We made our share. But we were determined that the mistakes we made in this new era would be passion-based and not fear-driven.

Our Anniversary Adventure

Deborah and I celebrated our twenty-fifth wedding anniversary by spending a few days in beautiful Victoria, British Columbia. The day we arrived I spotted a 1958 Vintage Beaver pontoon plane tied to the dock across the street from our hotel. It was available for tourists to take a flight over the island. It seemed to me that it was a great way to celebrate our anniversary, so I excitedly said, "Let's go for a ride." Deb was not so thrilled, but she eventually agreed, and we arranged to go the next day. We awoke to rather stormy skies but made our way to the plane anyway, thinking they would reschedule the flight. Much to Deb's chagrin (and my delight) they said we could go. So we climbed aboard and put on the headphones so we could hear each other. Soon our plane skimmed out across the bay and into the air.

Just so you get the picture, a 1958 vintage Beaver is about the size of a 1958 Volkswagen. It's possible to touch both sides of the plane at the same time. Deb sat in the back seat and I sat next to the pilot. As we gained altitude and headed over the island, the plane began to respond to a great deal of turbulence. The farther we went inland, the worse it became. We would later be told that we were in the air during the worst wind storm they had experienced in over thirty years.

Deb was starting to get a bit nervous and I was even wondering if this was such a good idea when the pilot's voice came through our headphones. "Are you guys alright with this?" Deb's response was a great illustration of our determination to follow after God, no matter how bumpy the flight. She boldly replied, "I'm alright if you're alright." The captain's next statement said it all: "Well, we've already gone past the point of no return; the best plan is to stay on course."

A Pastoral Change

Since the personality of a senior pastor often tends to attract similar personalities, we had a congregation that loved the

Lord and loved safely investigating His ways. They expected me to proceed the way I believed good stewardship demanded, which included planning the budget carefully in advance. It also meant spending hours on each sermon, entering the pulpit with every thought carefully written out. I didn't read my notes, but I depended on the Holy Spirit's ability to lay out the truths He wanted to convey ahead of time. And He put up with that, even honored it, for years, because He knew my heart.

Sunday mornings began to change, however, when we gave the Holy Spirit permission to make waves. When God began to seriously mess up our safe structure, some people took it personally. Friends left the church without even looking us in the eye to say goodbye.

We were severely tempted many times to return to the days of "nice church". However, God was faithful to lead us to places that became altars of covenant in our own hearts. These were points where we allowed the fire of the Holy Spirit to remind us that we had passed the point of no return. I'd like to tell you about a few of those altars.

Bonnie Bray Street

Our heart was with the treasure we had invested at the Los Angeles Dream Center, so the next year we took a group of board and team members to see the miracles with our own eyes. We marveled at the renovated hospital that was becoming a ministry command center and were stirred by outreaches like Sidewalk Sunday Schools.

While in the area, we took the opportunity to check out

the heart of the historic Azusa Street revival. There on Bonnie Bray Street about a dozen of us entered a run-down cottage. This site is recognized as the place of prayer that sparked a move of God in our country at the turn of the century. What we found wasn't a museum; it was a place still alive with the prayers of desperate saints. Within moments, all of us were face down on the floor in the heavy presence of the Lord. Every time I reflect on this story I experience the weight of His glory afresh.

At Bonnie Bray Street, we realized that we could never again settle for less than the weight, splendor, and magnificence of His presence. No matter how that looked, we were literally in it over our heads. Some people thought we were out of our minds, but it was too late; we were past the point of no return.

Florence, Kentucky

Throughout this faith journey, our friend Dan McCollam—now a vital part of our Resource Team at The Mission—has been a connector to many people and events that seemed both wild and wonderful. Dan was on staff with pastor/revivalist Cleddie Keith during this season. In 1997 we accepted his invitation to attend a leadership conference that became another milestone.

Pastor Cleddie had been crying out for a move of God for decades and he wasn't about to quench that move in any way. He decided long ago that the gospel was to be demonstrated, not just declared, and that the Holy Spirit was someone to be experienced, not just talked about. I'm telling you, things looked very weird; it was all way outside our experiential box. People were worshipping with abandon. Colored scarves and banners were being waved wildly, and no one seemed to care that there was little "order".

There were several guests speaking at this conference, and each of them helped bring revelation about what God was doing in us, but the greatest moment of truth for me came through Pastor Cleddie. It happened in the last service that we were able to attend before flying home. My personal fears had been increasing about the difficulties our present course of action was bound to bring to the church. And though I was committed to not going back, I felt like I was out on a very precarious limb listening to the sound of a chain saw.

It was then that Cleddie made the platform and altar area of the church available for those whose fears were challenging their resolve. My son Ryan and I quickly rose to our feet and found a place on the platform. As Cleddie prayed, God met us with His Holy fire and burned His courage into our faith. We came off that platform with an even greater resolve to go after God. The Decisions were being formed and refined in my spirit.

Fiji

Our first Fiji story actually started when Deb and I were in England at a conference presented by a new friend, Graham Cooke. That's a great story in itself, but I'm only mentioning it here because our connection with Fiji actually started while we were in England, and that was important to us. God was up to something much bigger than our physical presence.

On a Friday night while we were gone, Talatala Philimoni Kama Waqa, who was at that time the pastor of the largest church in Fiji and the leader of a network of churches, attended a Friday night meeting at our church with his nephew.

Upon returning home to Fiji, Pastor Waqa convinced the leaders of his church network that Deborah and I should come and be the main speakers at the next national church convention. He did this without ever hearing us preach! Later, when we asked him why he invited us, he said that they needed to hear from a pastor who would allow God to move in the way he had seen on that Friday night. He wanted me to bring Deborah because the Fijians had never seen a white woman dance before the Lord.

The invitation to minister in Fiji overwhelmed me with anxiety. When Pastor Waqa called to ask me to go, my first response was to delay so I could find a good reason to say no. But something was changing in me and before I could say "no" or "I'll get back to you", I said, "Yes".

Who Said That?

I was shocked. What had I done? I had spent twenty-four years of ministry taking the safe path at every fork in the road. Missions trips? Sure, I'd helped build buildings. But I'd turned down any invitation to speak, both in the States and abroad, telling myself that "my church needs me", or "there isn't enough money", or the ever popular "I have a check in my spirit". The truth? I was intimidated. But here I was volunteering to put myself in the position to fail. I was the most surprised man on the planet.

That first trip to Fiji was a whole different type of milestone in our journey. Deborah and I found ourselves being used in miraculous ways that honestly amazed us. It was in Fiji that we came to grips with the call on our lives to raise up a church that could make an eternal difference in the nations.

The unmistakable move of God in my heart put my fear where it belonged. I was becoming more afraid of disobeying God than of venturing out of my comfortable box.

A Dramatic Dream

We returned home from Fiji for just a week before we were to leave for Brazil, and in that week I had a dream. I was in the ocean. The water was calm and I wore something like a life vest. Although the water was vast, I knew I couldn't sink. I heard the Lord say, "Do you want to be in the middle of my will?" I said, "Yes."

The water became a little rougher; the question came again; and I said, "Yes," more strongly than ever. The waves became huge: the same question, the same answer. As a huge wake broke over me, there was a sense of danger, but security as well. I was screaming agreement in the dream, and woke myself up, saying out loud, "Yes, more than anything."

Our Resolve Is Tested

We had been invited to go to Brazil as part of the support team for one of Randy Clark's healing crusades. Randy is very well known and loved in Brazil because so many have been saved, healed, and delivered from demonic torment through his ministry. Tired of believing in healing and deliverance while seeing only a few healed or delivered we were anxious to watch, listen, and learn.

When we arrived at the airport, another new friend, Ricky Stivers, told us that Randy's flight had been delayed, and he wasn't going to be there that night. It was the first meeting of the crusade, and they expected about four thousand people, every one of whom eagerly anticipated hearing from Randy Clark. Rick said to me, "I think you're supposed to speak tonight." I laughed, sure that he was joking.

Deb and I checked into the hotel and were then taken to the venue. About five minutes before it was time for the preaching, Rick leaned over, looked me in the eye, and said, "Are you ready?" Something rose up inside, a strength I didn't even know was there, and I heard myself say, "Yes."

As I said "yes" the Holy Spirit spoke a few short sentences into my spirit. That was all I had as I walked onto the platform. Remember, now, we're talking about David Crone, a pastor who usually worked on every sermon for hours, afraid to speak anything that hadn't been planned in detail.

An Explosive Response

I went to the microphone and delivered the brief word. The word was short but it wasn't sweet—in fact, it was quite strong. But people immediately began to flood the altar. Shocked by the response, I turned to the interpreter and asked, "Did you say what I said?" He responded confidently, "Yes, I said exactly what you said."

Then I asked Deborah to come to the platform. She delivered another brief but powerful word, and the rest of the audience came to the altar, where all heaven broke loose.

This was, and still is, a defining moment in our lives, a moment where God showed us that He was in charge, and He wanted to use us in ways we had never imagined. There was no turning back. We were becoming Special Forces, not spectators.

Reflection Questions:

As you absorbed this chapter, were you reminded of pivotal points in your journey? Why not take time to lists your own points of no return? On the other hand, you may be recalling times God opened doors for you that fear kept you from walking through. He is the ultimate Redeemer and would love to help you prepare for the next faith adventure He has planned for your life. If you write a prayer now, you'll be able to look back at this day of decision and rejoice.

chapter
5

DREAMS AND VISIONS

"We have decided that hearing about the Holy Spirit without experiencing Him is silly, that believing in His presence without seeing it manifested in signs and wonders is hypocrisy."

"We have decided that reading about the book of Acts without living the book of Acts is unthinkable."

If we were chatting over a cup of coffee, this would be a great place to take a break so I could ask you some questions. I wonder, for instance, what the phrase we use in The Decisions, "Living saved but not supernatural" means to you?

If you grew up in a legalistic church environment, you might interpret living supernatural as a call to live a more externally holy life…a ban on watching inappropriate movies, for instance. While those choices are indeed important, they had little to do with how we saw this decision working out in our lives.

To demonstrate how this looked, I'd like to tell you a couple of ways God grabbed me personally and began to redefine my interpretation of living supernatural.

"Do Nothing 'Till You Hear from Me"

During the year we prepared to build the sanctuary, God taught me so much about hearing, obeying, and depending on Him. For months, the Holy Spirit would not let me talk to the congregation about the new building. The people knew we were preparing, but I wasn't allowed to make any special push for funds at all.

You can bet that I questioned whether I was hearing Him clearly. Was I making it all up? To me, it was a weird method of fundraising, but God was faithful to validate the fact that I was really hearing from Him. He began to visit me the way I'd read about for years in Acts 2:17: "In the last days, God says, I will pour out my Spirit on all people. Your sons and daughters will prophesy, your young men will see visions, your old men will dream dreams" (NIV).

I was somewhere between old and young when I began having both meaningful dreams and visions, and it really shook me up

It Wasn't the Pizza

In the first dream of this new season, I saw Deborah wearing a dress I'd never seen before. There were two pictures in the dream. In the first, Deb was standing with her eyes closed, praying out loud. She was standing over a woman who was lying on the floor with her head under a chair. In the second part of the dream, I saw Deborah in a fetal position on the floor near the altar. In both pictures she was wearing the same dress.

I got up and went to church early to speak in a pre-service meeting; Deb wasn't dressed for church when I left the house. By the time I came into the first service, worship had already begun and Deb was waiting for me in the front row. She was wearing the exact dress I'd seen in my dream. Shocked, I asked her when she got the dress. She thought I was upset about the dress, because I seemed so serious and I rarely notice what people are wearing. Of course, she found out later why I was stunned.

During the prayer time at the end of the first service, I turned from the person I was praying with to see Deborah standing near the first row, praying with her eyes closed. She didn't realize that the lady she was praying for had fallen to the floor with her head under a chair, just like I'd seen in the dream. You can probably guess that after the second service, I found Deb praying on the floor in a fetal position. Then I heard the Father say into my spirit, "I gave you a dream and brought it to pass in the same day. I did that so that you would know that what you heard in your spirit about the building fund was my voice and that I intend to bring it to pass." So much for normal, right? God was definitely upgrading His ways of speaking to me.

One morning, later that year, I was just waking up when I asked God how He was going to perform the promised miracle that would provide the funds we needed. He said, "I'll bring you a man." And he showed me a man. I couldn't see his face, but I noticed the pattern in the shirt he was wearing.

Bigger and Better than Our Dreams

The next Sunday, the Holy Spirit finally released me to talk about the new sanctuary and encourage the people to give. He was very clear that I was to tell them to mark the date as significant. Following the second service a man and his wife approached me to talk about the building fund. They revealed to me that they represented a foundation that looks for ways to bless the Kingdom and were interested in helping with our project.

When the man told me their foundation would match every dollar the church raised in the following year, I noticed he was wearing the shirt I'd seen in the vision. I'm telling you, the people who create reality shows for television know absolutely nothing about the Surreal Life; I was living it.

This is a small example of what living supernaturally looks like in our lives.

Reflection Questions:

You don't have to be a pastor in a building program to relate to this chapter. Are there storms in the sea of your life? Maybe the Holy Spirit is speaking to you about holding onto something you think is a life raft, but is really an anchor. Whatever the case, why not pause here to write your thoughts?

chapter
6

"YOU NEED HER"

"We have decided that having good programs is not enough, that change without transformation is intolerable, and that staying where we are is not an option."

"We have decided to be infectious instead of innocuous, contagious instead of quarantined, deadly instead of benign."

I honestly would have told you that there was nothing inferior about our marriage. While Deborah felt unusual and sometimes uncomfortable about the fact the she didn't play the piano like other pastors' wives she knew or fit the traditional pastors' wife image, I was as happy as one of the clams in her legendary cioppino, the Italian seafood soup for which Deb's famous.

That's a good analogy, too, because the clams in the soup are dead, which sets up the story of one of our first strange and painful God-inflicted marriage experiences. Back when all this started, Deb and I went through the same ordeal. We both felt that we were going to die. I mean all the way dead—physically—not just "mostly" dead. The experience was so unusual that we didn't talk to each other about it for a long time, but Deborah had actually begun to hide little notes under a few of her prized keepsakes, telling which child should receive that item as an inheritance after her death.

When we finally felt released to talk about it, we had to

laugh. But really, the Holy Spirit was getting ready to shift the very foundation of our marriage. He was not changing it; He was transforming it.

My New Wife...

To talk about what The Decisions did to our marriage, first I'd like to tell you about my uniquely gifted wife.

Deborah is a fantastic gardener: she mows the lawn, plants all the flowers and shrubs, and trims the hedges, too. She loves working with power tools and actually wants to receive such things as a chop saw or laser leveler for her birthday. Deb's an excellent interior designer who plasters walls and does professional grade faux finishes. Deborah is a great cook...a wonderful mother and grandmother...a terrific hostess. It's amazing.

In the old days of safe church, Deb's favorite way to serve the church was to stand watch at her post behind the information counter every Sunday, where she'd greet people until the singing started, and then slip into the service unnoticed. She usually sat on the back row so she could quickly return to the info counter for the next service. She was content to stay in the background resisting any attempts made to involve her publicly.

As I've told you, Deborah was first to have many Holy Spirit experiences, which was incredible in itself, since she'd always been so down-to-earth about all things spiritual. She was physically healed of several long-term physical problems—and that was just one result of an extended divine encounter with the Holy Spirit. Later she went to a conference and came home shaking violently from head to toe, and it lasted for hours. I watched in wonder. I was confused but certain that she, of all people, wasn't faking it. God was up to something, whether either of us understood it or not. I stood and watched, like a live lobster that didn't realize the cold water was gradually getting hotter.

Here Come the Prophets

Then there were the prophetic words that were spoken over us. At the beginning, we weren't even sure people could be called prophets in our time. Now we drew them like flies wherever God took us exploring. They would spend a long time talking to Deborah about what soon became a prophetic laundry list of promises. One common statement was "You will be an Esther and you'll influence heads of government."

The prophets would speak to Deb at length, and then almost always look at me and say, "You need her." Or someone would say, "Dave, you're going to have a global apostolic ministry, but you don't want to hear that..." Then they would walk away or turn to Deb and continue describing her prophetic destiny.

These people were not talking about the Deborah I'd known and loved since I was a teenager, and it took some adjustment. No, it required transformation. It wasn't that I wanted to retain a position of power in our marriage; it's just that it felt so uncomfortable and unfamiliar, like trying to write with my left hand. My wife's character was already superior, but if these unusual prophetic people were right, she was becoming, well, one of those unusual prophetic people.

And in what seemed like two or three seconds, the prophecies started to come true. Deb was receiving amazing revelation and was now willing to share it publicly. She began to powerfully minister to tormented people, with life-giving results. It was as if all the gifts and the abundant anointing God had packed into her life were now being released.

Renewal Gets Real

Theoretically I was thrilled. But practically I was not a happy man. God was using what He was doing in Deb to challenge my comfort level, expose my hidden insecurities, and unveil my wrongly placed identity.

I was not enjoying the Father's way of transforming me. What had happened to my wife? In the past, she had always been the one waiting for me to finish ministering; now I was waiting for her. I spent hours preparing a sermon that barely kept the man on the fourth row awake; then she stepped up to give a two-minute word that brought heaven down. "Hey," I wanted to shout, "I'm the Man of God here. Remember me? I'm the pastor. The prophets flock to her and walk away from me? You can hate me or love me, but don't ignore me!"

Deborah didn't seem to be much help at first. She was understanding things about herself that had mystified her for years, and for the first time in her life she was free to be the woman God made her to be. In all the joy she was experiencing, Deb was perplexed as to why I was having a problem. In my soulish emotional state, her advice to me sounded like, "I can't help you, get over it." Although this sounded like no help at all, it was exactly what I needed to force me back to my identity in Christ.

Now, the description of our conflict may be slightly exaggerated—but only by a miniscule measure. This was a season of intense pressure for both of us. But as the psalmist David discovered, the place of our distress was also the place of our enlargement. (Ps. 4:1)

Deborah and I met as young children and became sweethearts as teenagers. We have always been each other's best friend. But for the first time in our relationship we had to learn how to fight so that both of us win. We had to learn how to fight with each other and for each other, giving of ourselves to each other in a radical love. The process was grueling—but worth it.

As for both of us dying? I'm happy to be alive to report that we were only dying in areas of our flesh that were in the way of faith and intimacy. We've found our footing on higher ground, and no one is more proud of my wife than I am. She has taken her place in the army and is no longer simply a part of the audience.

Deb's Governmental Anointing

Before our first trip to Fiji, Deborah had a dream about four women where she saw the specific colors the women were wearing. When she woke up, she knew she was supposed to find fabric and make the scarves that matched their dresses, so she did.

We indeed encountered three of the four women in Fiji. Deb recognized them from her dreams, and gave them the scarves she had made. It was more difficult to present the final scarf, because it turned out that the fourth woman in her dreams was the wife of Fiji's Prime Minister, Mrs. Chaudhry. Due to security issues, we were unable to meet with her on that trip; but through her pastor, Deb was able to give her the scarf and a number of scripture references. Little did we know what a great impact those scriptures would have in the near future.

Shortly following our return from Fiji we learned that a violent coup took place there. A Fijian leader and several other armed men stormed the government building and held the Prime minister, his son, and other men in the Parliament hostage for over six weeks. Fiji hung on the edge of civil war while governments around the world withheld financial aid, devastating the nation's economy. Finally, through supernatural divine intervention, the coup came to a peaceful end. Prime Minister Chaudhry and the others were released.

The Rest of the Story

We heard the rest of the story on a later trip to Fiji. We were ministering with a team on the east side of the main island when Mrs. Chaudhry, at that time a member of Parliament, heard that Deborah was nearby. She sent a message to Deb and arranged to meet at the hotel where we were staying. Over coffee, she revealed the personally painful circumstances of the coup. On a number of occasions, her husband was taken out of the building for execution, with a gun to his head, only to be dragged back in and mistreated further. Her son had been so traumatized by the experiences that he required a lengthy time of healing following his release.

As Mrs. Chaudhry finished the story, she shared that the scriptures Deb had given her kept her strong and gave her hope during those trying days. She read those scriptures to her husband, during his captivity, when she was given permission to speak to him by phone. Here is a portion of one of the scriptures the Father gave Deborah for this woman: "May the Lord answer you in the day of trouble. May the name of the God of Jacob defend you..." Ps. 20:1 (NKJV).

That's my Father and that's my girl.

Reflection Questions:

There are a number of ways you may be reacting at the end of this chapter. Maybe you're not married and you'd like to express to God your desire to have this experience, with all its joys and challenges. Or perhaps the Holy Spirit is breathing hard on the old paradigms of your marriage, and it almost seems like it's the work of the enemy. Whatever your experience, I'd like to pray for you right now.

Father, You know that our dreams and decisions about marriage are some of the most important commitments of our lives. Guide my friends as they commit their hopes to you again right now. Let them know that You are the creator, refiner, and redeemer.

chapter
7

CONTENDING FOR THE CALL

"We have decided that we are a battle ship not a cruise ship, an army not an audience, Special Forces not spectators, missionaries not club members."

"We have decided that singing songs without worshiping is empty, and having meetings without God showing up is pointless."

It doesn't take a theologian to know that everything in the Kingdom must be contended for. Even our prophetic words are to be weapons that we use to bring about our destiny.

Deb and I were scheduled to return to Brazil several months after the trip I told you about in chapter three. Many people in our congregation had really put the brakes on our present course; things were not going well at all, and I knew it was not time to go on an international mission trip. Deborah and the team went without me.

During Deb's trip, both of us experienced a dark spiritual battle. The spiritual warfare in South America is blatant and hit Deb hard. When she called home, it was very difficult to hear what was happening and not be there with her. Meanwhile, the problems that kept me in Vacaville were still a dark cloud that remained with me day and night.

The wrestling between the need to deal with the local church problems and our burgeoning apostolic call to the nations was intense. It was just a year or so earlier that ninety-five percent of the church had responded to Graham Cooke's invitation by surrounding Deborah and I at the altar, affirming both our apostolic call and the call of the church to impact nations. Now it seemed they were withdrawing their affirmation and stepping back.

The War for Worship

Compared to the bigger picture, the issues that were keeping us from going forward in both of these calls seemed so petty and unwarranted.

One of the greatest conflicts in the church at this time centered on the worship. Some didn't like the style, others the volume, still others the songs themselves. Even the personalities of the ones leading the worship became an issue. This was no small battle and it touched every part of church life. It shouldn't have surprised us that one of the biggest battles we faced came in the same area that heaven itself had to deal with. Understanding this didn't make it any less painful though.

Deb and I came out of the difficult Brazil trip experience with a fresh resolve.

We determined not to despise the chastening of the Lord. I felt like many things that had happened were my own doing, not just people's wrong responses. Some things were a result of our lack of knowledge about how to make a corporate transition and pastor a move of God. We had failed a test, but I knew we would have another opportunity to address these issues. We embraced His correction with joy.

We also covenanted not to give the condemnation of the enemy a foothold. Every failure is an opportunity for us to fall prey to the enemy's accusations. It is also, however, an opportunity for God to display His outrageous grace. We chose the latter.

A Congregational Release

A year later, God gave us another chance to embrace our destiny. Deborah and I felt a real urgency to return to Fiji, even though we hadn't been formally invited by anyone except the Holy Spirit. I called Pastor Waqa and he insisted that we come. I told him I would only come if our church allowed it. At the end of a Sunday morning service, I told the people about this pressing internal call. I made it clear that I wasn't asking them for money; I just wanted their permission.

While I was talking, a woman stood and came up with money in her hand. She pressed it into mine, and said, "You can't rob us of the blessing of sending you." Then many people came forward and put money at our feet—enough to pay for the trip. The whole congregation stood and applauded in approval.

We all understood that this event was about much more than one trip to Fiji. The body was affirming our passion for global ministry and the church's call to impact nations. It wasn't the end of that journey, but it was a very important milestone.

Reflection Questions:

Is there any area of your life that is being slowed or stopped altogether by the fear of man? Or perhaps the inferior way that leads you astray is your disregard for those you love. Why not pause here and ask God for His perspective on this subject?

chapter
8

AUTHENTIC CHRISTIANITY

"We have decided that living saved but not supernatural is living below our privilege and short of what Christ died for."

"We have decided that gifting without character is futile."

The next stories may seem quite different on the surface; however, as you'll see, they all addressed similar areas that God wanted to upgrade.

Cars and Compromise

Another wedding anniversary was coming up soon, and I really wanted to get something meaningful for Deb, so I asked my daughter, Amy, if she had any ideas. She said, "Dad, the best gift you could give Mom would be to buy yourself a car."

Now wait, I know that sounds like a bad husband joke, but Amy was right. We'd sold my car and given the money to the building fund earlier that year. Because of my irregular schedule, my wife needed me to have my own car so that her life could flow more smoothly.

So I did one of my favorite things in the world…I went out to test-drive new cars. I often do that on my day off even when I'm not looking for a car!

One day, my Dad, our son Jeremy, and I went car shopping.

I found the car I really liked, a BMW Z3 convertible, but I told the salesman we'd keep looking. We found a larger, more conservative car, and I almost bought it. The two cars cost almost the same amount, and we could afford either, so money wasn't the issue. Jeremy stopped me cold when he asked me why I was buying the larger car.

I had to answer honestly. I told him that I was very hesitant about doing anything that might stir criticism from people who already disagreed with many of my choices. Since I'd even taken flack in the past about my vehicles, I was unwilling to take any more chances.

Jeremy looked me in the eye and said, "Dad, it sounds to me like you're making a decision based on the fear of what people will think. You need to get the car you want."

That little BMW convertible has been a lot of fun!

You Can Call Me David

This next story relates to a shift that happened when I told the church that my first name wasn't Pastor. They always knew that, of course, and I'd never insisted that anyone address me that way. In fact, one Sunday afternoon for lunch someone else had put in the pizza order for the group in my name, and when I heard, "Order for Pastor Dave" blaring over the intercom system, I was irked. I figure that when I get to heaven Jesus isn't going to say "Well, hello, Pastor Dave," so I don't need to insist on the title here.

During this time, however, I took this issue one step further when I began to formally ask everyone in our congregation to stop calling me "Pastor Dave" whenever the title separated me from them or elevated me above others. Permission was granted to call me Dave or David. If a person or a situation needs the title, that's all right. But my name is David.

Let me give you an example of the way this issue looks in my life. When we host conferences at our church, I'm usually not very visible, so I can sit down between sessions in our on-site café and simply talk to people. We'll be having a perfectly enjoyable conversation…they'll be asking questions about the church and sharing their spiritual journey. But then someone who knows me stops by and blows my cover, letting my new friend know that I'm Pastor Dave Crone.

The conversation immediately slides into a whole different mode, a proper mode that's much less real and far less interesting. Just a minute earlier I'd been getting to know someone, and they were becoming acquainted with a guy named David; my title changed that and that feels inferior to me, less than the best.

Say it Again

One Sunday morning not long ago, I felt I should affirm our shift away from titles. After the service a man who was new to our congregation came up to me and said, "While I was standing next to you during worship this morning, I really wanted to give you a hug, but the fact that you are the pastor stopped me." Then he grabbed me with enthusiasm, hugged me like a man set free and said, "Thank you."

Speaking about this issue to our church body was a bigger statement than first meets the eye, and I believe it goes back to the prophetic words that have been spoken over us. In my religious background, the only acceptable titles were Pastor, Brother, and Sister. We didn't call someone Missionary Smith or Evangelist Martin.

So when the prophetic people started talking to me about an apostolic calling, I couldn't even hear it. There was no paradigm for such a title or function in my religious history. But as the Holy Spirit continued to renew my mind, the push of those prophetic words stirred in me a realization that God was calling me to something bigger than a title, more important than a position.

The Holy Spirit was calling me first of all to be a son, and out of that identity to serve others. At times I am a neighbor, a friend, a servant, and a man who holds the door open for his wife's ministry and makes a place for the passions of his friends. Sometimes I am a local pastor, and at other times a person called to step up and affect global leaders apostolically. It began to be clear that these roles were all equally important in God's eyes and each one was a reflection of who I am in Him. Once again, God was letting us know that change without transformation is totally intolerable.

A Celebration in China

Here's an example that illustrates this paradigm shift from a vastly different angle.

In 2001, my family began to ask how I wanted to celebrate my 50th birthday, which was coming up in September. Did I want a big family party or an all-church celebration of some kind?

I thought and prayed about it. What came to the surface

was a desire to spend my 50th birthday doing something that was prophetic in its nature. Instead of celebrating my past, I wanted to declare my future. I specifically hoped to spend my birthday washing the feet of an apostolic leader in the persecuted church: for me, that meant China.

One Sunday morning I told the congregation about this desire. A friend came to me after the service and said that if I was serious, he knew someone who could arrange the trip. Between the ability of the Holy Spirit to expedite plans and the benefits of the computer technology, plans were in place by the end of the week.

If it's in Your Heart...

When it came time to purchase the tickets, I wasn't so sure this was the will of God. Having searched the internet for the best flight and prices, I sat with my finger on the mouse ready to click "buy"—but I couldn't do it. So I asked Deb to come into the office, and I asked her, "Do you think this is the will of God? Should I really do this?" Her answer was of no help: "If it is in your heart, do it." And she walked out of the room. I called her back in: "Deb, come on, help me here, what is your sense about this?" Same answer, same exit from the room. I was getting frustrated by this time and my finger ached from hovering over the mouse button. So I pulled the prophecy card. "Deb, come in here and tell me what you think. You're the prophetic one. You prophecy to others, you can at least prophecy to me." Expecting an intuitive response, I watched as she left the room reciting her now familiar mantra—"If it's in your heart do it". I got it. With a "click", the ticket was mine.

Two days later on a Sunday morning, I was interviewing a man that has spoken to more world leaders over his lifetime than any Christian leader alive today. He knew nothing in the natural about my desire to go to China. I asked him, "How many leaders have you witnessed to?" He started to answer my question then pointed to me and said, "You are going to China and you will speak to leaders in the underground church."

What a moving, humbling experience it was for me and my son Ryan to meet and subsequently spend my 50th birthday with ninety leaders of the house church movement. It was a dream come true to find myself literally washing the feet of the apostle responsible for starting two dozen mission stations To put that into context, a mission station was defined to us as a group of thirty-thousand believers.

Wake Up Call

Those dear people have paid such a high price for their calling. Most have been imprisoned and tortured repeatedly, yet that has only caused the zeal of their faith to burn more brightly. The first morning after we reached our destination, Ryan and I were awakened around 4am by a loud noise. We learned that Chinese Christians habitually rise early to storm heaven. They were singing "It's 4 a.m. in China", a song written by a young Chinese girl who has written over a thousand hymns sung all over China. The sound of their passionate singing and tearful prayers was both humbling and inspiring.

Whenever I am tempted to fall into the mold others would put me in, or find myself settling for an outward expression instead of an inward conviction... When I look to a title for an edge in a situation or my head begins to rule my heart... I only have to reflect on these three stories. They remind me to be true to myself, keep my identity in Christ, and respond to the Lord first from my heart. In other words, I choose to live authentically in the freedom that Jesus paid for on the cross. Living less than that is not an option any more.

Reflection Questions:

As you read this chapter, did you think of roles that may have restricted you in the past? If so, is this a new line of thinking or have you been frustrated about a format for awhile now? Perhaps this chapter caused you to rethink the way you view your own pastor or church leaders. This might be a great time to write your thoughts.

chapter
9

A NEW TEAM PARADIGM

"We have decided to value both pioneers and settlers: pioneers to expand our territory and settlers to build on those territories. But we are not squatters, people who take up space others have fought for without improving it."

In 2001, we went through a very painful time of parting with five dear friends who had held positions of ministry at our church, some of them since before I became the senior leader. There had been so many changes in who and what we were as a church it seemed we were stuck and unable to move forward. I knew that changes needed to be made in personnel for the sake of the church and the individuals. In looking for a way to move forward, my only paradigm was to release them from their paid staff positions at our church so that they could find other places of vocational ministry. This was not a unique approach; it is how most of the church world operates.

Though I attempted to do this in the best possible way, it became a time of turmoil that was painful for everyone. The individuals that were asked to leave, people within the church who loved them, and the staff members that remained were all hurting. Out of this experience came a determination that we had to find a better way to live together in ministry and never make such a transition the same way again.

We longed to learn how we could help the people with

whom we shared life, walking them through to their destinies, joining with them in their exploration.

As we began to work through this, God honored the direction we were taking even before we knew how to begin to achieve our goal.

A Prophet Comes to Vacaville

One person who has been especially instrumental in our relational shift is Graham Cooke, a prophet from England.

After many years of feeling a call to base his prophetic ministry in the States, Graham felt that God was finally releasing him to do that on a half-time basis. He had established great relationships with various American churches and their leaders, and he had offers to settle several places.

During Graham's season of transition, we had several meals with him, visited him in England, and invited him to minister in the church. In time, a mutual friend approached Deborah and me to see if it might be possible for Graham to make Vacaville his home base in the States.

When we spoke face to face with Graham, we offered him the only things we had: office space and our friendship. Graham accepted our offer. He told us later that we had offered him the one thing he was looking for—friendship.

We made room and created an office for Graham and his personal assistant. We've since carved out space for his media mailing center and a storage area for his books and teaching CD's, which are ordered and sent all over the world.

This was the kind of transition I was looking for. It was

based on relationship, friendship, common vision, and destiny.

The relationship has been a mutual gift to us here at The Mission as well as to Graham and his team.

This is significant because one of the other desires the Holy Spirit has imprinted on my heart is a call to make room for ministries that will be resources for the church globally. This sometimes means providing physical space and always includes relational support to friends who are moving into ministries that are not "normal". The easiest way to explain this concept is to give you some examples of the resource ministries that find their home at The Mission. So we'll tell you how they look, at least as this book goes to press. Graham keeps reminding us that we are in a divine season of latitude and indulgence. Plans seem to be upgraded weekly!

The Test

Two years after our painful separation with former staff members, we were given an opportunity to test our new resolve.

In 2004, we began to sense something different happening in the destinies of four friends who had been part of our in-house pastoral team for years. Three of these friends are now members of our Resource Team. Their transition from holding "staff" positions to becoming part of a regional and global resource is significant. As I shared at the beginning of this chapter, we had determined that there had to be a better way of dealing with transition. So when we again recognized that a shift was needed, we asked better questions and came to some powerful conclusions that have energized the church and allowed individuals to follow their passions and destiny. Since we had become friends together in kingdom living, our questions centered around finding the true call of each individual and how to help each one fulfill that call.

Dan McCollam

Dan McCollam started ministry as a member of "King's X", a Christian hard rock band, and went on to wear many hats as an associate minister. While still serving as one of our staff pastors, Dan embraced the renewed outpouring of the Holy Spirit and impacted many churches around the world with freedom and joy. In 2005, he transitioned from a paid staff position to more fully engage his life mission of restoring indigenous worship music. His passion is expressed around the world through a ministry called Sounds of the Nation. Another church in Vacaville, The Father's House, led by our friend Dave Patterson, has also invested themselves in this unique team ministry. Dan still ministers regionally, stoking the continued fire of the Holy Spirit, as well as teaching musicians how to write worship songs.

www.iwarschool.com.

Tim May

Tim May had led everything from singles to seniors, as well as serving as publisher of a church newspaper. One assignment he reluctantly accepted early in his ministry was to pioneer a new prison ministry. Much to his surprise, that has become a consuming passion for Tim. He now leads Ebenezer

Ministries, which takes the gospel to prisoners and is based at The Mission. Tim has raised up teams that go into local prisons weekly, as well as speaking and singing at regional prisons. One branch of Ebenezer's outreach is the One Voice Praise Choir, a group of singers from several Vacaville churches that present Spirit-led concerts in various regional prisons and churches. Tim has many invitations to influence the prison system both nationally and internationally.

www.ebrock.org.

Joyce Milton

Joyce Milton was also part of our paid staff. She served the single's ministry for a season, as well as teaching women's classes, counseling, and overseeing children's ministries. Her true passion was for writing and releasing the creative gifts in others, so in 2005 she embarked on an adventure that is still being defined. She loves to bring joy and encouragement to leaders around the world. She's also in a writing school, learning how to tell the stories so those who serve God faithfully can be honored, encouraged, and uplifted more widely in prayer.

www.live2laugh.com.

Paul Barber

Paul grew up as a teenager at The Mission. After graduating from Bible College he joined our staff to assist the youth pastor, later serving as the youth pastor for over ten years. Paul's passion to see kingdom life invade every area of society led him to move to Phoenix, Arizona where he is a successful business man. Paul continues to speak into the life of The Mission through his relationship with team members. He recently accompanied me to the Philippines where we worked with young leaders. Paul's transition was uniquely important to us as we continued to shift in how we viewed "ministry".

Taking a High Road Together

Walking these four "pastors" through the transition to their true passions has helped us find a way to do church differently. Dan, Tim, and Joyce remain on our leadership team but are funded largely through outside resource ministries. Their time is given to their primary passions, yet we continue to walk in friendship and community within the church. As these three long-time staff members shifted to what we call our "resource team," others were drawn to The Mission also. They've become part of a relational team where ministries aren't just based out of the church but flow in and out of local kingdom life in a strategic life exchange.

It's been a real joy—and very humbling—to see God bring these excellent ministries to The Mission, and to join their journeys, as well. I can't take time to tell you about all the resources that are connected with us now, but here are two that will give you a taste of what's happening...

Byron and Crystal Easterling

The Easterlings relocated here from Texas in 2004. Byron is a prophetic minister who travels globally, building relationally through "Build His House" ministries. Byron and Crystal are people of prayer with real servants' hearts. www.bhhinc.org.

Bill and Carol Dew

Bill and Carol moved from San Diego to Vacaville, where they have balanced traveling with Randy Clark, holding their own ministry and training conferences, as well as serving in the prayer, deliverance, and healing ministries of The Mission. They carry an unusual anointing for bringing people into the manifest presence of God.

www.dewnamis.com.

The Dews Try to Move On

I'd like to end this chapter with a story that is a significant example of this paradigm change in team relationships.

We met Bill Dew when Randy Clark came here to hold his first healing crusade. Bill came to meet Randy and eventually became part of Randy's traveling ministry team. After traveling with Randy for eighteen months, Bill and Carol trained healing teams for Randy's crusades, as well as ministering to people in his international meetings. They settled in Vacaville in 2000 and became a part of our resource team.

In 2004, the Dews asked to meet with Deborah and I, so we went out for lunch. As we talked, they told us about dreams they'd been having and prophetic words they'd received about a soon-coming season of transition in their lives. It was a very dry season in their ministry; their calendar contained far too much white space, and something needed to change. Bill is an action-oriented person, and we soon realized that they'd already come to the conclusion that it was time to move on, ending their connection with The Mission.

It was one of those, "Things that make you go 'hmmmm…'" moments. The Dews weren't angry or upset; they had simply taken the information they had and come to a decision on their own. It just didn't seem right. It did seem familiar, but it did not fit the way we wanted to live in this new relationship paradigm, so we asked them to meet with the extended leadership team to talk things over.

The Team Huddles Together

Soon after, a group of us met around the big kitchen table at our home. The Dews presented the same set of facts they'd told us at lunch. Graham Cooke asked, "Are you telling us or is this up for discussion?" Bill answered with a hesitant, "Yes, we are telling you."

We really are a prophetic company and we all care about the Dews. As a team we were unwilling to let their decision stand without discussion. We didn't want control of their decision; we wanted to see them live out their God-given destiny. So we began to ask questions that led us to a different conclusion than their original one. They were in a transition, but not the one they first anticipated. By the time that meeting ended, Bill and Carol committed to go home and pray about staying with us.

As I watched that discussion, I determined that things had to be different with our team from then on. No one would be a Lone Ranger, and Deborah and I would not be the only ones who helped people make major decisions. This was a very important landmark, because it set in motion the way we would deal with destinies in the future.

Since that time, God has made a way for the Dews to purchase a home in Vacaville, despite soaring San Francisco Bay Area real estate prices. Their ministry calendar is full and includes such God connections as a trip to Japan that was way beyond their normal box.

Reflection Questions:

Is there a dream in your heart that seems to be out of the question? What would you do with your life if finances weren't a factor? Are there people in your life that perhaps you need to include in your decision-making process? Why not take time to write about the issue that's alive in your heart right now.

chapter
10

THE SIGN OUT
BY THE STREET

"We have decided to be Holy Spirit filled, Holy Spirit led, and Holy Spirit empowered—anything less doesn't work for us."

"We have decided that teaching the gospel without demonstrating the gospel is not enough. Good preaching, good doctrine, and being good people are not enough."

For many years, our church housed a Christian preschool and elementary school. I believe Christian schools are wonderful and can be a real service to the community as families are impacted by the truths that children learn along with their scholastic skills.

But letting the Holy Spirit be the real chairman of the board meant that everything was on the table and up for discussion according to this one high standard: Is this the very best dream God has for this church?

As a leadership team we discussed this decision at length. It became clear that while having a school was a good thing, it wasn't our call. We knew that God had a call on our campus, not just for our formal church meetings. We had already started a school for adults, founded by our friends Curt and Susie Klein, who were then pastoring in the nearby town of Dixon. The Potter's House, our discipleship school, had already outgrown the Dixon facility and needed to move to Vacaville.

Our Changing Campus

We realized that if we had full use of the classrooms that were currently taken up by the grade school, we would be able to expand the Potter's House, hold other adult schools, and expand our Sunday School to reach children more effectively.

All these proposed uses reflected our spiritual DNA more accurately, so we bit the bullet and announced the closure of the grade school in 2004. I was pretty sure what we could expect. The biggest impact would not be in our own church, since most of the students in our school came from families that were active in other churches in our town; parents in our church were far more likely to be home schooling their children.

Still, the children in the school had become like our own family. Closing or moving the school meant an involuntary change for these children and their families, and I was concerned for the impact this transition would have. I was also concerned about the staff personnel that had faithfully ministered to these children for many years. They would need continued employment doing the task they loved. These concerns created no small conflict in this pastor's heart. I knew we had to follow the leading of the Holy Spirit, but what about these people?

God is Never Late

We had hoped that on the day of the formal announcement of the school's closure, we would be able to tell the parents where the school would be relocated, but nothing we tried for relocating the school had worked. Understandably, not all the parents took the decision well, nor did they hear our hearts. We have discovered, however, that the best decision is to be willing to look like you have failed in order to go after the greater thing God is calling you to.

One week after the difficult announcement, the Christian grade school merged with another successful school in town. They offered to keep the students together and promised employment opportunities to each of the staff members.

Prophetic Promises Come to Pass

Since then, the Potter's House has flourished. The school was too small at that time to pay a full-time teacher's salary, so Curt Klein resigned the Dixon pastorate and supported his passion for the Potter's House during the 2003-2004 school year by working at Wal-Mart™. I can't tell you how much I admire that choice.

In 2005, Phil and Sue Loyd, who came to Vacaville in 2001 with six of their children and no job prospects, led the first second-year program at the Potter's House. Every year we have more international students and more people come from all over America to learn and "do the stuff" every day.

In May of 2006, fifty people from the school invaded the island of Fiji where they witnessed the lame walk and the blind see. It was like living the book of Acts. A worker on one of the resort islands where the students spent a day reported, "If those people had stayed here for a week we would have had to turn our swimming pool into a baptismal pool."

A New Name

For the citizens of our city, the next changes probably just meant that there was a new sign out by the street as they drove by, the one that announces the name of our church and our school. For us, though, the changes were more far-reaching.

First, let's talk about the name change. When Deborah and I first became the pastors here, we were a denominational church called Vaca Valley Christian Life Center. It was a long title that always felt awkward.

We'd been affiliated with our denomination for a long time, and it had also began to feel awkward. I really don't want to spend long addressing this, but since it is an important result of the new decision-making process we've walked through, I'll give you the short version.

As Deborah and I began the process of discovering what God had for this church, we were increasingly exposed to other church streams and networks, along with their leaders. Our hunger for the presence of God had us exploring anywhere and with anyone contending for the same thing, inside and outside our denominational relationships. This was a new experience for us as we had stayed within our denomination most of our ministry.

I have often described this process of exploration with this image: Most of my ministry I was in a house called by the name of my denomination. Then one day I opened a door and found that I was only in a room of that house, whose real name is "The Kingdom of God." Having discovered this, I couldn't help but open the doors to the other rooms and see what was inside. What we found were many new relationships we would often describe as "those of our own tribe".

The Effects of Exploration

My limited exposure to the greater Kingdom was not the fault of my denomination, but the result of my own lack of seeking that Kingdom first. However, our adventures outside the denomination, along with other changing values, did begin to affect our relationship with the leaders of our regional governing body and our participation in their programs.

Our regional leadership had difficulty celebrating many of the things we have come to embrace, such as the five-fold ministry, especially the ministry of the apostle and prophet. Though at times they voiced disapproval, they often demonstrated great patience with us and we felt for a long time that we could continue to honor their leadership and stay connected governmentally.

However, relationships that are not nurtured soon begin to be less than healthy. God began to speak very clearly to us about not having affiliations without relationship. He made it clear that in continuing to stay connected without giving ourselves to the values of the denomination, we were operating with a lack of integrity and treating our leaders with disrespect.

As the leadership team, the board of elders, and the church body began to seek God for the way forward, we became convinced that dropping our affiliation and becoming a non-denomination church called The Mission was the will of God. This was confirmed by an overwhelming vote of the church membership.

This action made little to no difference in the way we did church; it was simply more authentic to what we had become. We continue to love and bless those we have known and counted as friends for many years while we were serving with that denomination. We pray only for God's very best in that movement and each pastor personally.

Ministry Around the World

One of the bigger internal changes reflected in our new name is the way we approach the outreach mission of the church. One of my frustrations over the years has been in functioning under the traditional method of missions. Mission was seen as ministry in other nations, making a distinction in the minds of churches between local, regional, and international ministry. This distinction inferred that there are missionaries and then there are the rest of us. It produced many people who believed that they fulfilled their mission by sending a few dollars to those that did the stuff.

Traditional global missions in our denomination looked like this... you sent your money to an organization that distributed it to a missionary; you received a newsletter every once in a while, and if possible had the missionary speak once every four years in the church. The lack of relationship and accountability in this system left the local congregation acting more like a bank than a companion in ministry, and, in my opinion, treated the missionary like a hireling.

New Mission Values

In order to address what we saw as an ineffective and dishonoring way to go about impacting our community and the nations, our leadership team proceeded to develop a set of mission values. These values include the following:

- We value the work of local, regional, and global mission equally.

- We value a priority on relationships.

- We value a common vision, which includes the pursuit of the manifest presence of God, the release of the power of God in signs and wonders, the recognition of the five-fold ministries described in Ephesians 4:11-13 as the manifestation of a kingdom mindset, and the commitment to equipping and empowering people to fulfill their kingdom destiny and ministry on earth.

- We value strategic life exchange.

- We value mutual accountability.

Following these values has moved our church from one that only sends money to missionaries to a church that produces missionaries. A much larger portion of the church is now involved in mission locally, regionally, and in many nations of the world. We are developing a culture of mission that has the potential to advance the mission of Jesus Christ across the street and around the world.

The sign on the street says "The Mission". The call and culture of our church community is beginning to say the same.

Reflection Questions:

As you read about this process, did the Holy Spirit refresh His call for you to make some hard, unpopular choices? Maybe you are in the middle of reaping results for choices God has called you to make. Take a few moments and write a prayer about the season you're in.

chapter
11

FRIENDS

"We have decided that having faith without works is not enough and having works without love is not acceptable—that our function comes out of our relationship first with the Father and second with each other."

I was a pre-natal church attendee, so I know how church life works, or doesn't. My parents were always involved in leadership as volunteers so I saw all sides of church relationships, including the one between the pastor and the congregation.

One of the "rules" of pastoring that became evident to me was the one that said pastors should not develop strong friendships with people in their congregation. I later heard this echoed in pastoral ministry classes in Bible College. This rule was confirmed in my early years of ministry, when I discovered that people often wanted to be my friend because I was the pastor, as if it gave them some social leverage. Along with this evidence, there seemed to be good logical human reasoning behind this philosophy, so I came to believe that this was the way it had to be.

That changed when we were marked by the Holy Spirit's redefinition of excellence. I came to realize that following that isolated way of living as a leader produces only function-based relationships that leave the pastor and his family, especially his wife, isolated and lonely. In a subtle way, existing on a relational island was living below our privilege and short of what Christ died for, and we were no longer willing to propagate those inferior values.

Well Worth the Risk

Having good friends within the community of believers you have given your life to may be risky, but when the Holy Spirit turned my life right side up, I knew I desperately needed people. And like so many other things in my life at that time, the cost didn't matter.

Raised in a healthy family and being blessed with great parents, a wonderful wife as a companion, and three children that filled my life, I have always required few outside relationships to satisfy my social needs. Now, with my family having grown to add two daughters-in-law, one son-in-law, one adopted son, and six grandchildren, my cup of social activity and meaningful interaction is beyond full. But one thing I learned about relationships through this journey: along with family, friends are not optional; they are essential.

When we first began to venture out in developing friendships, we realized we had a lot to learn about being a real friend. We knew how to have casual acquaintances and working relationships, but not true friendships—the kind that are made for adversity. I wasn't very good at it and made a mess of some of the most meaningful relationships we have ever had. I am so thankful for those that refused to stop loving me.

As I mentioned in the introduction, the stories in this

book are told from my perspective and they are my stories—Deb and I lived them. But we didn't live them alone. In fact, without the friends that have been in our lives, these stories would not only lose their meaning, they would not exist. If it were not for a community of friends hanging together in desperate pursuit of God's presence, I would be somewhere else selling used cars or real estate, dreaming of what might have been.

Significant Examples...

During the time when Deb was in Brazil and I was home wrestling with my own human fallibility, I reached a point that I can only describe as the dark night of my soul. I tried to pray, and found the heavens to be brass. My attempts at worship were wooden and lifeless. One day at home, I found myself overwhelmed with a feeling of isolation. I began to believe that I was going to be in this emotional turmoil the rest of my life.

At that moment, a friend showed up at my door. I had called the church office to let Dan McCollam know I was going to stay home; when he heard the sound of my voice, he decided to come to our house. It wasn't really anything he did; it was just that he was my friend and he was there. By the time he left, I knew I wasn't alone and I was going to get through this time and be stronger for it.

When circumstances seem unsettled, I often pull out a little slip of paper I carry in my Bible, where it has remained for nearly ten years. Written in a friend's handwriting are the words, "Dave, I believe in your dream", along with the scriptural reference, Isaiah 48:18-19. It was while I was sitting in the second balcony of Tommy Barnett's church, struggling to understand the dream God was giving me—really questioning whether anyone else would see it's value—that Curt Klein, a long time friend and colleague, handed me that little scrap of paper without speaking a word. That scribbled note continues to be a source of great encouragement; his friendship remains invaluable.

Board Members Become Real Friends

It's not often that you hear a pastor tell you that some of their most valued friends are the board members of the church, but you are hearing it now. The men serving on our board of elders have provided steadfast support during times of great turmoil. Their vision to see that God was doing something unique and wonderful in the midst of the mess of reconstruction made space for what we now enjoy. They are men with the wisdom to know that when God is on the move, you don't channel the move—it channels you. Here is one incident that illustrates this...

As my international travel increased, I wanted to make sure I was being accountable about where I was going and how often, so I proposed to the board members that they determine the number of Sundays I could be gone each year. Their response amazed me. They refused to cooperate with what I thought was a reasonable request. They made it clear they were confident that the call on my life to the nations was the call of the church and by restricting my time they would be limiting the possibilities. We agreed instead upon a partnership. I would let them know of the places I believed

I was to go, and they would be faithful to tell me if they felt a check in their spirits. It was an agreement among friends.

What a Difference a Friend Makes

Friends who are made for adversity, friends who are up for the fight—willing to fight for you when you can't fight for yourself—are indispensable in this pursuit of the manifest presence of God. Deb and I have been privileged to have friends who have loved us when we failed them, challenged us when we were settling for less, and identified the best in us when we couldn't see it. They have filled our lives with timely phone calls, encouraging notes, prophetic declarations, and engaging conversations. They give The Mission its personality and character. The Mission is rapidly becoming a community of friends, and it doesn't exist for me without them.

Before I finish this chapter I want to say that friends outside our immediate church community who are going after the same things are essential also. They help give perspective when things get crazy and you wonder if you're really hearing from God. Friends of this nature, whose hearts are to see heaven invade earth, have helped us keep our equilibrium in rocky times and our eyes on the goal.

If it is true that a man with friends is a wealthy man, I am prosperous indeed.

Reflection Questions:

Perhaps you'd find it helpful to spend a few moments reflecting on the impact your friendships have had on your life. Are you too isolated? Or maybe your house is Grand Central Station, a place where no one has a chance to recharge. What's the Holy Spirit saying to you about this vital subject?

chapter
12

DREAMING WITH GOD

"We have decided that nothing short of His Kingdom coming and His will being done in our world as it is in heaven will satisfy."

At the start of the 2005 Potter's House, Deborah and I were sitting with the first-year students sharing some of our life story, when a revelation dropped into my heart and a whole new adventure began. Deb was telling a story about our courtship and the day I proposed to her and how surprised she was that I was willing to give up my bachelorhood. She knew that since I was a young boy I dreamt of traveling with some kind of ministry and that marriage would complicate things.

I had heard her share this story many times before and have always enjoyed the pleasure that the memory evoked. This time, however, it dawned on me that I was now living the dream of my youth. In that moment I realized that for nearly twenty-four years my dream had been shelved by the responsibilities of family and church, but not forgotten by God. He hid the dream in His heart, let it grow, then gave it back to me with a dimension greater than that nineteen-year-old youth could have imagined.

Caught Off Guard

The revelation that God cared about the dreams of my

childhood so caught me off guard that I broke down in front of the students with uncontrollable emotion. They stared at me, probably wondering why this 35-year-old story would bring me to tears and second-guessing their decision to come to a school led by an overly emotional middle-aged man. Deb was perplexed and I was embarrassed, but the truth is I was devastated by the goodness of God.

Exploring God's Abundant Love

The journey to this revelation started two years before in an interesting place: the underground church in Northern China. Dan McCollam and I had traveled to a city near the Mongolian border to meet in a small apartment with about twenty-five house church leaders. In order to protect these leaders from persecution, we had to teach eight to ten hours each day in whispers so that our voices would not be heard outside the room. In one of our teaching times, we gave the leaders an exercise in hearing the Holy Spirit speak to them through a specific passage of Scripture. We had them meditate on Paul's prayer in Ephesians chapter three and record what they heard the Holy Spirit say to them.

I participated with them in the exercise by focusing on the last part of the prayer where Paul exclaims, "Now to Him who is able to do exceedingly abundantly above all that we ask or think, according to the power that works in us" (Eph. 3:20, NJKV). As I meditated, I began to get a picture of how big the dimension Paul described as beyond "all that we ask or think" really is. I sensed I was being invited by the Holy Spirit to explore this unknown and expansive territory. It struck me that this is the arena of the supernatural and it seemed to have no limitations. It is the place dreams live.

Tricked

Just as I was reveling in the possibilities of the impossible I heard what I thought to be the Holy Spirit say, "But you know the limits of your personality." At first I agreed, but then I became angry and responded, "That's not fair! You made me with this personality and you can't limit my dreams just because of the way you chose to make me." As my consternation continued to rise and my arguments became more emotional and less logical, I heard the Holy Spirit laughing as if to say, "Gotcha!" Jehovah Sneaky had goaded me into stepping out of my own limited mindset and stepping into the place of dreaming dreams bigger than myself: above and beyond what I could ask or think.

In the months following that embarrassing moment standing before the first-year students, we began to explore with our company of friends at The Mission the freedom to dream. One of the most significant moments in the evolution of our church took place when Deborah and I stood before the people and gave them permission to dream their own dreams.

Granting the church permission to dream has set us on a path of unlimited possibilities. Childhood dreams, crucified by the realities of life and the limiting words of significant adults, are being resurrected and breathed on by the Holy Spirit. Artistic expressions of many kinds are being discovered and released—photography, painting, writing, song composition, recording, and sculpting, to name a few.

Businesses with a kingdom agenda are developing, and creative ways of ministering are being explored.

Latitude and Indulgence

The full potential of all this is yet to be seen. In fact the word "potential" is no longer adequate since it suggests that there is a ceiling, a limitation. This place of dreams is the territory of possible impossibilities.

We are beginning to discover that God was not kidding when He said through the psalmist, "Delight yourself in the LORD and He will give you the desires of your heart" (Ps. 37:4, NIV). He wasn't talking about heaven when He moved Paul to write, "Eye has not seen, nor ear heard, nor have entered into the heart of man the things which God has prepared for those who love Him" (1 Cor. 2:9, NKJV). He loves to dream with us and use those dreams to reveal himself, bringing transformation.

One of the exciting fruits of developing this dream culture in the church is that people are joining together and encouraging each other's dreams. We call it a new way of "fighting with each other". People are finding ways to partner in their journeys, and as a result, we have discovered a fresh atmosphere of unity that resists an unhealthy competitive spirit. We are contending for unity by contending for the dreams of our friends.

Graham Cooke has prophesied that we are living in a time of latitude and indulgence. It's a time when God has granted us permission to explore our dreams with wide latitude and a time in which God wants to indulge himself. We are finding this to be true and can sing with the psalmist, "We were like those who dream. Then our mouth was filled with laughter, and our tongue with singing. Then they said among the nations, 'The Lord has done great things for them'. The Lord has done great things for us and we are glad" (Ps. 126:1-3, NKJV).

Reflection Questions:

If you are full of gratitude for dreams that are coming true during this season of your life, why not stop and write a prayer of thanksgiving right now?

Or it may be that you have dreams that have been crucified by time and responsibility? Are they lost or just hidden in God's heart, growing in the incubator of His possibilities? How might your resurrected dreams look?

chapter
13

THE DECISIONS AND YOU

"We have decided to be the ones telling the stories of God's power—not the ones hearing about them."

"We have decided that we will not be satisfied until our world cries out, "Those who have turned the world upside down have come here too" (Acts 17:6, NKJV).

Right now, as I write this, I feel a lot like the character Kevin Costner played in one of my favorite movies, "Field of Dreams". All kinds of bizarre things happened to him, events he could only tell his wife, but he built a baseball field on valuable land even though that meant sacrificing part of his cash crop—stalks of corn so tall a kid could get lost in there for days.

He did this because he had heard a voice saying, "If you build it, they will come."

I can relate.

We have built it: a large sanctuary that is completely paid for. We are building it: a group of friends who have bought into each other's passions and dreams. We will build it: whatever God says, however He wants it constructed, whatever He wants to produce.

They have begun to come. From places like Florida, Texas, Minnesota, the United Kingdom, India, Fiji, and Romania, they have come, not knowing what God has in store, just answering God's call.

They haven't all arrived, either. We're experiencing very healthy growth, but as I write this, I'm pretty sure that there will still be some empty seats in our sanctuary the next time I preach at The Mission. That breaks my heart, because people need what Jesus died to give them.

But God's word has always proved true, and we believe that His promises will come to pass. I could fill another book with the prophetic words given to our church over the past few years, and we are doing our very best to walk in the joyful obedience that positions us to see every prophecy fulfilled.

Gideon's Warriors

The first time we met Graham Cooke, he prophesied that God was developing our church into a Gideon's three hundred (Judges 7:7). This was not good news to me; it sounded like reduction. If the ratio of those that stayed in relation to those that left in Gideon's army was the same ratio in our church, attendance on Sunday morning would only include our family—and not all of us at that.

This prophecy soon became a word of encouragement as the Holy Spirit began to talk to us about Gideon and the men He chose to face the enemy.

The people of Israel were living under the oppression of other nations. They were living in caves for protection, and every year their crops and livestock were stolen. Even Gideon, this great man of valor, was hiding in a wine press, afraid to winnow the wheat out in the open. All of this would change when their enemies were defeated and everyone in the nation would benefit from the victory. They would enjoy hearing the amazing stories for generations to come.

We Want to Tell the Stories

But Gideon and these three hundred men would not only benefit from the freedom, they would be the ones to tell the stories of things others never saw. They would be the ones sitting around the family dinner table or standing in the city gates describing the indescribable feeling of being in the middle of a miracle, while others would only be able to wish that they had been there.

Here at The Mission we have embraced our destiny to be a people like Gideon and his three hundred men and decided to be the ones telling the stories. The miracles are happening and the stories are being told.

We will make more mistakes, because we're human, we're learning, and we haven't passed this way before. But we are not a company of those who shrink back in fear. We are convinced that staying where we are is not an option. Our hearts have been sealed and stamped by the Holy Spirit. We have decided that we will not be satisfied until our world cries out, "Those who have turned the world upside down have come here too"(Acts 17:6, NKJV).

Reflection Questions:

Have you realized, as you read these stories, that you have stories of your own to tell? What about the promises God has given you, stories yet to be told? Take time to note them here even if God has yet to fulfill His word—because He will!

chapter
14

THEREFORE...

"We have decided that we are a mission station and not a museum."

O ne of my college professors would often say, "When you come across a 'therefore' you should always find out what it is there for." Our "therefore" is there for defining our decision to be a mission station and not a museum.

When I read the words of Jesus to Peter declaring that he would build his church and the gates of hell would not prevail against it (Matt. 16:18), I find it impossible to imagine that he had in mind anything that resembles a museum.

A museum is defined by the American Heritage Dictionary as, "An institution for the acquisition, preservation, study, and exhibition of works of artistic, scientific, or historical value."

A museum is a place where things are collected, gathered, stored, and displayed in order for us to view, contemplate, gain knowledge and perspective, and to appreciate what has been. It reflects the culture and society that it represents, and displays its history. Its goal is to educate and inspire.

Transforming a Culture

All of this is good. I personally enjoy visiting museums and have been at times emotionally impacted as well as educated—but never transformed.

In contrast, the goal of a mission station is not to reflect the culture but to transform it, not to display its history but to determine it.

The mission stations of the early history of California were far from museums. They were outposts of destiny. Their primary purpose was two-fold: they were to claim new territory for the nation of Spain and change the spiritual culture of the people in the region. Once established, missionaries would be sent out to plant a new mission, thereby expanding the territory and increasing their spiritual influence. This led to a system of missions all up and down the coast of California.

Though the mission system in California became corrupt and was used as a political tool by the Spanish government, the basic idea in its purest form illustrates the nature of the Kingdom of God, of which the Church is a part. Jesus said the Kingdom is like yeast that starts small but leavens the whole loaf of bread (Luke 13:21). It invades the territory and changes the makeup or culture of the dough. This is what we believe Jesus had in mind when he made that declaration.

On our first trip to the UK, Graham took us to tour Warwick Castle. It was first established around 1,000 AD and its original purpose was much like that of a mission. Its primary functions were warfare, expansion and protection, as well as farming for provision. A community developed around and in the shadow of what would become an impenetrable fortress. In all the centuries of warfare experienced by England, the walls of Warwick Castle were never breached.

Much later in its history, the castle lost its original purpose and became a place where the nobility and royalty came to play. It hosted parties and diversions for the rich and famous. It was not long before it became what it is today—a museum, a monument to its history, lost to its destiny.

As we stood on the walls of that castle, we were convicted by how easily the Church has often followed the same pattern and become so unlike the destiny Jesus had in mind. We determined then that the church God planted us in as leaders would not walk down that inferior path, but by the grace of God would set its course to go from glory to glory, and ever increasing glory—to hear Jesus say when he looks at The Mission, "Now that's more like it."

Therefore...

We have decided that we are a mission station and not a museum.

We honor the past, live in the present, and keep our eyes on the future.

We focus on what could be, not on what is or has been.

We see past events—successes and failures—as stepping stones not stop signs.

We pursue learning in order to be transformed, not learning in order to know.

We are not limited to the four walls of our church building. Our influence is not restricted by location—not even the nations are out of bounds.

We are more concerned about how many we send out into the world than how many we convince to come into the building. The number of people we have or do not have in our building will not be the measure of who we are or the measure of our effectiveness.

We raise up world changers—not tour guides. We train commandos, not committees.

We are people of engagement, not observation.

We are people of our destiny, not of our history.

Therefore… We are "The Mission".

My Prayer for You:

Father, thank You for what You have done and all You are about to perform in our lives. I pray that the person holding this book in their hands would sense Your call to the way of excellence. Show them what that means in their lives; guide them with Your eye. Thank You for the stories of our lives.

Give us an ever-growing spirit of wisdom in the knowledge of your Son and keep us hungry for your presence. May your Kingdom come to each of us, and may your will be done in my life and in the life of the one reading this book, as it is in heaven.

In Jesus' Name, Amen.

personal
decisions

personal
decisions

personal
decisions

personal
decisions

personal
decisions

personal
decisions

To order additional copies of this book,

please visit:

www.tmvv.org/decisionsbook.html

Made in the USA
San Bernardino, CA
13 October 2016